God
Safari

Seeing God
in the Rhythms
of Nature

by Rhoda Gerig

Preface

My first trip to Africa began out of a mourning process. For me I was mourning the loss of my mother. My friend, who came with me, was mourning the loss of her husband. We had walked with each other in the process of those deaths. I also was recovering from cancer treatments and multiple surgeries so we were both in survival mode. My friend and I would call each other to talk to someone who understood, to tell the other what a rotten day we had. It was a running joke that we would crown the winner of whoever's day had been the worst. At some point during that time, we both decided that we needed something to look forward to. That is when we decided to plan a trip to Africa.

I still remember the morning of the first week that we were in Kenya when we had the conversation about how great it was to get up in the morning not dreading the day but expectant of what new wonder we would see as we went out on a game drive. That trip changed me. It flipped a switch from waking up thinking about how to survive a day to waking up expectant of what the day could bring. It also changed the way I look at the common things around me. Back in the U.S. I was driving home from the airport and I passed a field with a deer in it. To myself I thought, "Oh…ho hum…a deer. It's not nearly as exciting as a giraffe." But as soon as the thought had left my mind I also thought, there's probably someone in Africa looking at a giraffe and thinking "ho hum…just another giraffe." I decided then that any day I wanted to go on a safari I could do it here at home. All I had to do was change my mindset and go out expectant and look for what the day could bring.

My hope is that these devotionals will help the reader face life with expectancy, daily become more aware of the wonder of the natural world around them and allow it to point them to the creator of this fascinating world in which we live. God created this world with so many reminders that it isn't a world to just survive but one in which to thrive. One cannot look at the sheer varieties of what God created without realizing that it was made to give us joy.

I'm not a biblical scholar. I don't have a degree in biology or animal science. What I do well is watching and looking at details. Being a retired art and math teacher with a photography hobby has refined my skills at finding those details. I've read that the original word "safari" in Kiswahili means to journey or travel. My journey to Africa 14 years ago taught me to look at things in a different way. My journey to Africa this year has made me realize how blessed my life has been because of that change. So, I invite you to go on a God Safari with me looking for those details in nature that point us to God. Hopefully our differences will be bridged by the world and God we share.

Rhoda Gerig

My first trip to Kenya 2009.
I'm in front with my friend Janet

Focus

I recently heard this quote from Lysa TerKeurst, "We steer where we stare." This made me laugh because when I drive, I often find myself coming close to going off the road because my attention is focused on some animal or bird. As I watch an African Fish Eagle sitting on a perch, I see the same thing. As it looks for a fish it stretches its head one way and another as it decides where it's going to fly next. When it finally decides, it leans its head and the whole body follows as it launches from the branch. In flight when it is going to bank to the right or the left, its head will point the direction it's going before the body follows, until ultimately its talons find the fish.

As I've thought about the quote more, I just keep coming back to the importance of our point of focus. It has everything to do with where we end up. I do realize that sometimes all we can do is survive and the idea of looking for God in our daily lives seems like it is just too much work on top of everything else. But I do believe one of the ways to get beyond survival even in those times is by deciding where we will put our focus. God has given us many gifts that we often walk by and miss. Whether it's a sunset, a song we hear or a caring comment, there are many ways he gives us tiny bits of light even in the darkest of situations to provide the hope we need to hold on.

Philippians 4:8 (NIV) **"Finally, brothers and sisters, whatever is true, whatever is noble, whatever is right, whatever is pure, whatever is lovely, whatever is admirable—if anything is excellent or praiseworthy— think about such things."**

Creator of Light

Two of the wonders that God gives us daily is a sunrise and a sunset. I'll have to admit I've seen many more sunsets than sunrises because I'm not a morning person but to me there is nothing more peaceful than watching that sun sink below the horizon in the evening.

Light was the first thing that God created. Genesis 1:3-5 (NIV) **"And God said, "Let there be light," and there was light. God saw that the light was good, and he separated the light from the darkness. God called the light "day," and the darkness he called "night." And there was evening, and there was morning—the first day."** God, a timeless being, creating time. Since that first day there has been a sunrise and sunset.

The sunrise and sunset are a constant reminder of our creator God who spoke the light into being on that very first day. The consistency of the sunrise and sunset is a reflection of the consistency of the one who created them. James 1:17 (NIV) **"Every good and perfect gift is from above, coming down from the Father of the heavenly lights, who does not change like shifting shadows."**

Next time you see the sunrise or the sunset take a moment and thank God for creating them and for the twice daily reminder of His presence.

"From the rising of the sun to the place where it sets, the name of the Lord is to be praised." Ps 113:3 (NIV)

Speechless

There are some things in nature that are so amazing they leave you speechless and clearly point to a creator God. Usually, it is something large and grand that makes us feel that way but sometimes it's something small and detailed. Outside of Naivasha I had the privilege of watching a Black-headed Weaver bird build a nest. It is amazing to see as it starts with a few strips of grass attached to a branch which are then woven into a circle. From the circle the bird then adds on more grass tightly interwoven to create a round nest that is big enough to hold the eggs and once hatched, chicks. The detail of the nest is so intricate it's hard to conceive of how they can make it especially since all they have to do it with is their beak. Not only that but different types of Weavers have different nest designs. I can't look at all that detail without believing this doesn't happen randomly. Clearly God has his hand in it.

His creation speaks of his greatness. In the book of Job, even God, points to his creation when he answers Job's cries and questions. Actually, God doesn't answer Job's questions, he asks him some questions of his own. Job 38:1-4 (NIV) **"Then the Lord spoke to Job out of the storm. He said, 'Who is this that obscures my plans with words without knowledge? Brace yourself like a man; I will question you, and you shall answer me. Where were you when I laid the earth's foundation? Tell me, if you understand.'"**

God goes on to ask Job if he was there for each day of creation of the earth when he created day and night and separated land from sea. Then he points to lions, mountain goats, fawns, donkeys, oxen, ostrich, horses, locust, hawks, eagles and it goes on until finally concludes with this question in Job 40:1-2 (NIV), **"The Lord said to Job: 'Will the one who contends with the Almighty correct him? Let him who accuses God answer him!'"**

Job's response, Job 40:4 (NIV) **"I am unworthy—how can I reply to you? I put my hand over my mouth."** Job was speechless. The truth of nature that points to God can do that to you, leave you speechless.

A Timeless Moment

Have you ever had a timeless moment? For me those moments happen when I'm out in nature. When I got a chance to see flamingos at Lake Elementaita after photographing them for a while I just stopped and watched. It was too much to take in. As I sat there surrounded by such beauty, time just stood still. There aren't many places in my life where I feel like that. I don't often allow space in my schedule for it to happen because so much else seems to demand my time.

As a science fiction fan, I have always been fascinated by the idea of time travel or places where time does not exist. The idea has been explored in numerous TV shows, movies and books. I think one of the reasons that we as humans are fascinated with this idea is because there never seems to be enough time. Some of this desire comes from the self-important drive to find satisfaction in our daily lives, but I believe the root of this desire was put there by God. Eccles 3:11 (NIV) **"... He has also set eternity in the hearts of men."** This desire for timelessness draws us to him.

Until we reach heaven, I believe God gives us earthly glimpses of eternity, a little bit of "heaven on earth." Look for those chances God offers to us to "**Be still and know that I am God.**" Ps 46:10 (NIV) We can enjoy God's creativity with all our senses and allow time to stand still. The trick is making the time.

13

What's Your Part?

The African Harrier Hawk has something that makes it different from other hawks, it has double-jointed knees. This specially designed feature allows it to be able to squeeze its feet into nests on rock cliffs to find eggs and chicks to eat. I got to see this first hand as I watched a hawk land on the cliff in front of me and try to find something in the nests. It came up empty which was fine with me because even though I know life and death are a part of nature I'm fine with not seeing it, but I was fascinated by the hawk's special design.

God has designed us, as well as animals, with specially designed abilities. 1 Cor 12 gives us an illustration of this when it talks of the church being like the body of Christ. Each part has a special design and purpose. Each part needs the other parts to do what they were designed to do. No part is more or less important or powerful.

1 Cor. 12:24-27 (NIV) **"... But God has put together all the parts of the body. And he has given more honor to the parts that didn't have any. In that way, the parts of the body will not take sides. All of them will take care of one another. If one part suffers, every part suffers with it. If one part is honored, every part shares in its joy. You are the body of Christ. Each one of you is a part of it."**

Have you given thought to what your special design is within the body of Christ? Do you wish you were designed differently? Are you wondering if you really have a special purpose? It's not always obvious at first but start by asking God to show you your special purpose. It might be something you think of as simple or not important but remember that He may have just made you double-jointed for a reason.

Looking Below the Surface

For the first couple of weeks of my trip to Naivasha I would go to bed and no sooner than I'd turn off my light I would get dive bombed by moths. Other times they would wait until I was just drifting off to sleep and then land in my hair with a thud. While I knew they weren't dangerous it was still rather unsettling. I finally figured out that the light outside of my door was attracting the moths and I found a way to keep them out.

One afternoon I was taking a break from editing photos and saw a Nobel Swallowtail butterfly that was making the rounds of the flowers below so I got out my camera and took some photos. I clearly valued the butterfly with its pretty yellow color much more so than I did the drab moths that pestered me each night. But if you look at the purpose of a moth and butterfly, in nature, they both do the same things. They are pollinators and also a food source for many insects, reptiles and birds. The butterfly is just active during the day while the moth is during the night but both provide value in the interconnectedness of nature. The appearance is what makes the butterfly more valuable to a photographer.

It is easy to make judgements on the value of a person by their outward appearance and miss their inward value. In 1 Sam 16:7 God sends Samuel to find a replacement for Saul the king of Israel. Samuel is sure he has found the anointed one but then God gives these words, **"But the Lord said to**

Samuel, 'Do not consider his appearance or his height, for I have rejected him. The Lord does not look at the things people look at. People look at the outward appearance, but the Lord looks at the heart.'" (NIV)

Taking the time to look beyond the surface is something that allows you to see people through a different lens. And while we may not be able to look at the heart the same way that God can, the curiosity we show to go beyond the surface with others is a way to show them God's love.

Living Water

When visiting the Soysambu Conservancy we pulled over when we saw a Waterbuck and a pair of Gray Crowned-Cranes. As we watched, we noticed them walking to a muddy, almost dried up, watering hole, looking at it and walking away. Then we noticed them go to a concrete trough, look in it and walk away. Soon after we watched a big male Baboon, some Impala, an Eland and a group of Zebras all do the same thing. It was the dry season and with all the animals showing up at the same time it became obvious that this must be the normal time of day that the conservancy turned on the water for the animals to drink. For some reason on this day no one had come to turn it on. We were able to call the conservancy and as we were leaving, we saw someone coming to turn the water on.

It got me thinking about how important water is to the animals and to our survival. Where I live, water is plentiful so it isn't something I think about much. In Kenya, at the end of a dry season, it's very obvious. It makes me think of Psalm 63:1 (NIV) **"You, God, are my God, earnestly I seek you; I thirst for you, my whole being longs for you, in a dry and parched land where there is no water."** or Psalm 42:1-2 (NIV) **"As the deer pants for streams of water, so my soul pants for you, my God. My soul thirsts for God, for the living God. When can I go and meet with God?"**

or John 4:14 where Jesus is speaking to the woman at the well, **"…but whoever drinks the water I give them will never thirst. Indeed, the water I give them will become in them a spring of water welling up to eternal life."** (NIV)

This idea of water is a theme throughout the Bible. Water is so elemental to life. The living water that God offers us is too. Do I thirst for God with my whole being like the animals daily coming to that water trough?

Connections

I am struck by how many connections there are between the animals I see in Kenya. The oxpeckers that hang out on giraffes or cape buffalos and eat ticks and bugs off of them. The interconnectedness of the great migration of zebras who eat tall grasses, that make way for the wildebeest who are pickier and eat only shoots of shorter grass. The birds that follow the herds for the insects they kick up as they migrate. The crocodiles and predators that depend on the herds as they migrate to get a meal.

It reminds me of the way we were built, with the need for connection. While many of the animals in the examples above often ignore each other most of the time, they still need each other because of that connected part that helps them survive. God did not make us to do everything ourselves, he made us to need each other. In Genesis 1, God creates man to dwell with him and then in Gen 2:18 says, **"It is not good for the man to be alone. I will make a helper suitable for him."** (NIV)

God then made woman, from the rib of the man, creating a special connectedness between man and woman. Really if you look at the whole of the Bible the theme of our relationship with God and with each other is throughout. In fact, Jesus, when asked what the greatest commandment was, answered, **"'Love the Lord your God with all your heart and with all your soul and with all your mind and with all your strength. The second is this: Love your neighbor as yourself."** Mark 12:30-31 (NIV)

Hebrews 10:24-25 speaks to the how that connectedness should work with our brothers and sisters in Christ, **"And let us consider how we may spur one another on toward love and good deeds, not giving up meeting together, as some are in the habit of doing, but encouraging one another— and all the more as you see the Day approaching."** (NIV)

The Bible even ends with the final connection between God and his people, a wedding scene in heaven in Rev 21:3 where it says, **"Look! God's dwelling place is now among the people and he will dwell with them. They will be his people, and God himself will be with them and be their God."** (NIV)

As you go through your day look for those opportunities that God has given you to connect.

Reflections

Reflections are something, as a photographer, I'm always looking for. They add so much to a photo. I'm always hoping for very still water so the reflection is a mirror image. There are times that you will have some reflection but the water is moving due to wind or an animal or bird disturbing the water which makes the reflection less perfect. I got a few reflections of birds getting drinks out of the Malewa river, some of Flamingos at Lake Elementiata, even a Bushbuck reflection but the thing I was hoping for was Zebra's reflections as they drank. I finally had the opportunity at Nairobi National Park as we were heading out. We stopped at a pond and sure enough some Zebras came to drink. Of course, the Zebras going into the water disturbed it so the perfect reflection didn't happen but the reflection of stripes on the Zebras make for some interesting photos.

That imperfect reflection makes me think of the verse in Proverbs 27:19 (NIV) **"As water reflects the face, so one's life reflects the heart."** How often is the reflection of my life made imperfect by ripples in the water? And what causes those ripples in my life?

The great news is we have the hope of knowing that God is transforming us into his perfect image. 2 Cor 3:18 (NKJ) **"But we all, with unveiled faces, beholding as in a mirror the glory of the Lord, are being transformed into the same image from glory to glory, just as by the Spirit of the Lord."** Transformed into the same image, that is hard to even imagine but definitely something to reflect on.

God Will Provide

I was taking photos of the place I was staying, outside of
Naivasha, so that I could show my friends back home. I started with
a photo of the house and then down by the river where I was
photographing birds. I also took one from another deck higher up
which showed more of the river but until I went to the top of the
property, I really didn't have the whole picture. As I stood on the
highest deck that overlooked the property, I realized my
understanding of the whole area was not complete at any of the
lower areas. They only gave me a piece of the picture.

Our church did a sermon series on a book called "The Story"
which was the Bible in story form without marked chapters and
verses. The thing that stuck with me from this series was the idea
that in any Bible story there is an upper and lower story. Look at
the story of Abraham and Isaac, when God tells Abraham to
sacrifice his long awaited, beloved son, there is nothing in the
lower story that makes sense.

In Genesis 22, God instructs Abraham to take his own son to be
sacrificed. At the last minute, God provides a ram caught in the
thickets as a substitute sacrifice, a foreshadowing of God giving his
son Jesus as a sacrifice for our sins. But the story loses its suspense,
agony and potential cruelty when we know the final outcome.
Take a moment to imagine being asked to sacrifice your own son.
Imagine Isaac, who was old enough to carry the wood for the
sacrifice, old enough to question his father about the missing lamb,
imagine what was going through his head. This passage takes place
over three days. Three days in which I'm sure both had agonizing

24

questions that were met only with silence and the choice of whether or not to obey God.

As much as I want to neatly wrap this story up with a bow, sometimes God doesn't let us in on the upper story and all we can see are a few pieces. What I can say is it is about relationships, trust and obedience. This wasn't the first time Abraham trusted God. When God asks Abraham to **"Take your son, your only son, whom you love"** in Gen 22:2 (NIV) it has to be a heart wrenching thing for Abraham to do. But he also had a love for God who had proven himself, over a period of time, to be trustworthy. Love isn't logical. Love is a commitment beyond the comfortable. Love trusts and makes us willing to do things that don't make sense. Abraham trusted there was an upper story (a heavenly view) which made sense whether he understood it or not.

The story ends with a ram provided by God. Gen 22:14 (NIV) "**So Abraham called that place The Lord Will Provide. And to this day it is said, "On the mountain of the Lord it will be provided."** Would I be able to be as obedient as Abraham? I don't know but I do trust that God would either provide the strength to do what he asks or would be able to provide a way out. Either way, because of years of my relationship with God, I know he will provide.

Delight

As we headed back from a trip around Lake Naivasha, we stopped the boat for a bird I had only previously seen in wildlife shows. They would always put funny music with the video of this bird hunting. The Black Heron will put its feathers out in front and over its head, in an umbrella shape, shading the water. A fish seeking shelter from the sun will then be eaten. The heron looks quite comical as it continuously moves from place to place doing this. I had no idea these birds even were in Kenya so I was quite delighted to find out there was one right in front of me. Comical birds always make me happy and I was delighted to see its humorous behavior as it fished.

Delight is defined as great pleasure or to please someone greatly. The Bible speaks of delight in many places. Ps. 37:4 (NIV) says, **"Take delight in the Lord, and he will give you the desires of your heart."** Also Ps. 112:1 (NIV) says, **"Blessed are those who fear the Lord, who find great delight in his commands."** It seems a bit easier to delight in the Lord than to delight in his commands. But if we truly delight in the Lord, the desires of our heart will be His and delighting in His commands is a natural outcome of that.

One of my favorite verses with delight in it is Zep 3:17 (NIV) **"The Lord your God is with you, the Mighty Warrior who saves. He will take great delight in you; in his love he will no longer rebuke you, but will rejoice over you with singing."** God takes delight in us. He rejoices over us with singing. He is with us. That's so much better than a comical bird.

The Dance

While watching Flamingos, on Lake Elementaita, I saw something I had only previously seen on nature documentaries on TV. I got to see the Flamingos do their mating dance. It was a sight to see as they walked in synchronized steps while clustered together all standing tall with their heads stretched upward. Scientists aren't sure if this dance is how they choose their mates or not because no studies have been done. But they do believe the color that the Flamingos display during mating season is a factor in choosing a mate. The more vibrant feather color at breeding time comes from a combination of what the Flamingos are eating and the more frequent preening which spreads an oil through their feathers making the color brighter.

I can't help but see the parallel to our Christian lives. We need to be aware of what we "eat" or in other words, what we feed our hearts and minds. Do we set our focus on "things above" as Col 3:1-2 says? **"Since, then, you have been raised with Christ, set your hearts on things above, where Christ is, seated at the right hand of God. Set your minds on things above, not on earthly things."** (NIV)

Just as the flamingos "clothe" themselves by enhancing their color by preening. In Col 3:12 it goes on to say, **"Therefore, as God's chosen people, holy and dearly loved, clothe yourselves with compassion, kindness, humility, gentleness and patience."** (NIV)

And if I'm not pushing the analogy too far Col 3:14 is like the unity shown when the Flamingos dance together in one group. **"And over all these virtues put on love, which binds them all together in perfect unity."** (NIV)

This dance of perfect unity doesn't happen overnight but as we focus on things above and get to know our Savior and his "unforced rhythms of grace" we "learn to live freely and lightly." Matt 11:30 (MSG) **"Learn the unforced rhythms of grace. I won't lay anything heavy or ill-fitting on you. Keep company with me and you'll learn to live freely and lightly."**

Breathtaking

I only have to look at the skies to see evidence of God. On my flight home from Kenya, I saw the most incredible, breathtaking, cloud formations. Ps 19:1-4 speaks of the heavens, **"The heavens declare the glory of God the skies proclaim the work of his hands. Day after day they pour forth speech; night after night they reveal knowledge. They have no speech, they use no words; no sound is heard from them. Yet their voice goes out into all the earth, their words to the ends of the world."** (NIV) They need no words to speak of God's glory.

A cloudless night sky is just as breathtaking. I was able to see a full moon rise while in Naivasha. It was a beautiful sight to see. Ps 8:3 says this of the night sky. **"Look at the splendor of Your skies, Your creative genius glowing in the heavens. When I gaze at Your moon and Your stars, mounted like jewels in their settings, I know You, God, are the fascinating Artist who fashioned it all!"** (TPT) I love that this translation refers to God as an Artist. Think of all the art where the subject matter is just a copy of God's creative work, as is my nature photography.

I have always loved this verse in Col 1:16-17 for the line **"in him all things hold together."** Here's the whole verse, **"For in him all things were created: things in heaven and on earth, visible and invisible, whether thrones or powers or rulers or authorities; all things have been created through him and for him. He is before all things, and in him all things hold together."** (NIV)

After a recent sermon at church, I love that line even more. Our pastor was talking about all the different things that have to be just right for life to exist on earth. For instance, if the earth's axis was tilted just a bit more life wouldn't exist. If the earth spun just a little faster on its axis life wouldn't exist. If earth were just a little bit closer to the sun life wouldn't exist. He went on to say that there are 150 different scientific constants that if they were just a little bit off then life would cease to exist. **"In Him all things hold together"** literally. As I look at the sky I am amazed by its vastness and if he can hold all of that together, he certainly can hold me too.

Prepared

While at Selenkay Conservancy outside of Amboseli, I was hoping to get to see the lions that were in the area, especially knowing they had cubs. It was fascinating watching the guides look at paw prints trying to locate the lions. The first night, we were unable to find the lions but did the next morning. Again, we had to rely on the skills of the guides this time to get us in a good position for photography. As we drove through the bush, we had to lean into the center of our vehicle so the thorns didn't scrape us. It was a bumpy ride but our guides got us in front of the lions, in great light, without disturbing their natural behavior, three different times. It was one of those perfect times where everything comes together just right. But it was not without effort and planning.

Preparation is what made that moment possible. The guides prepared by learning the signs the lions left behind to be able to track them. They learned the lion's habits and behaviors. They learned the landscape and the lighting so they could figure out how to get us in the best position to take photos of the lions. I had done some preparation too, getting the right camera equipment, learning the settings and features on the cameras which would produce the best photos. Not to mention all the preparation by the camp staff, preparing a place to stay and food to eat.

1 Peter 3:15 tells us that we should be prepared, **"But in your hearts revere Christ as Lord. Always be prepared to give an answer to everyone who asks you to give the reason for the hope that you have. But do this with gentleness and respect."** (NIV) When I read this, I notice three things that have to happen before I give an answer. I have to be prepared. I have to have hope visibly showing in my life so the person will ask. And they have to ask. I don't think any of those things happen without me living constantly revering Christ as Lord. Daily realizing that he is in charge, ordering my days and being open to the Spirit's promptings as I come in contact with those I meet.

Light

For my first boat ride on Lake Naivasha, I got up early to get there for the morning light. Photography is all about the light and while you can take photos without great light it isn't usually worth the effort. If you have too little light photos are just dull and listless. Too much light and you have dark shadows. Soft morning light or late evening light is the best. The light that morning was so perfect and there were so many birds. Getting up early was definitely worth it.

The way I think about the word "light" changed when I read a book that was looking at Einstein's Theory of Relativity. Einstein said that at the speed of light there is an "eternal now." I don't really understand much about that theory but I do know that without an obstruction the speed of light will go forever at a constant speed, a forever constant--an eternal now. God chooses to introduce his son, who is both eternal and never changing, as the Light of the World (John 1:9)

Also in John 1:1-5 he is called the Word and the Light of all mankind, **"In the beginning was the Word, and the Word was with God, and the Word was God. He was with God in the beginning. Through him all things were made; without him nothing was made that has been made. In him was life, and that life was**

the light of all mankind. The light shines in the darkness, and the darkness has not overcome it." (NIV) When you see that beautiful morning or evening light let it remind you of the Light of the world. And when the world seems dark, remember the eternal, never changing Light, and know it will not be overcome by the darkness.

Wilderness

I've had very little experience with areas that I would consider wilderness so, when the Bible talks of the wilderness, I can only imagine what that is like. I won't have that problem anymore because when we drove to Amboseli from the Selenkay Conservatory we went through what I can only say was a wilderness. It seemed to go on for miles just barren land, no trees just the sight of Mt. Kilimanjaro in the distance and an occasionally dead animal carcass. While at Amboseli's marsh we could watch dust devils form in some of those dryer areas off in the distance. On the ride home through the wilderness area we got to experience a dust storm for a few seconds as we drove through an area where the dust was swirling. You had to close your eyes and mouth to keep the grit out. Thankfully it was over quickly and soon we were back to the camp.

When I think of that experience and then think of the Israelites who were out in the wilderness for forty years, I have a new appreciation for what that would have been like. While the wilderness is a place we would like to avoid, it does seem to be a place where God shows up and prepares people for their next steps. God spoke to Abraham in the wilderness. He spoke to Moses through the burning bush in the wilderness. God met Elijah in the wilderness and in the desert, God called John the Baptist. Even Jesus went to the wilderness before starting his ministry.

While the wilderness is something I'd do anything to avoid, there is something about the lack of distractions and the fragileness of life in the wilderness which makes it easier to hear God's voice. If you are feeling like you are in the middle of your own wilderness, keep listening. Isaiah 43:19 (NIV) **"See, I am doing a new thing! Now it springs up; do you not perceive it? I am making a way in the wilderness and streams in the wasteland."**

Eagles Wings

I heard them for several days before I saw them. African Fish Eagles were just upriver from where I was staying. I was told they came and perched in the tree just outside my door but it was six days before I saw one fly over. By the next day, after a boat ride on Lake Naivasha, I had so many African Fish Eagle photos I was not nearly as eager to go take photos when one showed up right outside my door. But of course, I still did.

American Bald Eagles are something that are common in my area and I have taken thousands of photos of them over the years and I have yet to get tired of watching them. They are so powerful and graceful in the air and so funny when they walk on the ground. I've spent countless hours at eagle's nests waiting for the eaglets to take their first flight only to watch them crash land. Landing takes longer to learn than flying. Watching eagles feeds my soul.

I am so familiar with eagles that when I read a Bible verse with eagles in the verse, I immediately picture an American Bald Eagle. But after this trip to Kenya, it got me thinking about different kinds of eagles. In fact, as I thought of it and in my mind replaced my Bald Eagle with a Fish Eagle I thought, wait, there are other eagles too. So, whether you think of Fish, Martial, Long-crested or Tawny when you read these Bible verses, I've given you your choice of photos to help your imagination. They all are the perfect illustration to uplift and feed your soul.

"Praise the Lord, my soul;
   all my inmost being, praise his holy name.
Praise the Lord, my soul,
   and forget not all his benefits—
who forgives all your sins
   and heals all your diseases,
who redeems your life from the pit
   and crowns you with love and compassion,
who satisfies your desires with good things.
   so that your youth is renewed like the eagle's."
   Ps 103:1-5 (NIV)

"But those who hope in the Lord
   will renew their strength.
They will soar on wings like eagles;
   they will run and not grow weary,
   they will walk and not be faint."
   Isaiah 40:31 (NIV)

Family

It is a fantastic sight, seeing the elephant families come single file towards the marshes of Amboseli. The intensity of the sun creates heat waves which adds even more to the mystic of watching these gentle giants. The marshes where they eat have too much salt in the water so the elephants have to go elsewhere to get water which creates this "parade" every morning back to the marshes.

I think one of the things, besides their sheer size, that draws me to elephants is their family relationships. In fact, our guides knew all the different family matriarchs and each of their offspring by name. They could tell you the family history too. Other animals show family connections but are often difficult to keep track of once their offspring grow up, where elephant families stay together with the exception of the males.

Family relationships are often a mixed bag for most people, some good, some bad. But families are important because they shape who we are. A Christ follower has two families that can help shape them, their biological one and the family of God. 1 John 3:1-2 (NIV) says, **"See what great love the Father has lavished on us, that we should be called children of God! And that is what we are! The reason the world does not know us is that it did not know him. Dear friends, now we are children of God, and what we will be has not yet been made known. But we know that when**

Christ appears, we shall be like him, for we shall see him as he is." We are being shaped to "be like him."

The amazing thing is, God can use the good and the bad in our relationships to help us to "be like him." As I look back at some of the bad that was in my family, it was the process of dealing with it which actually provided the most growth. Thankfully some of the growth has also come from the encouragement of others. Heb 10:24-25 (NIV) says, **"And let us consider how we may spur one another on toward love and good deeds, not giving up meeting together, as some are in the habit of doing, but encouraging one another—and all the more as you see the Day approaching."** As you go through your day give thanks for those who have encouraged you and look for ways to be an encouragement to others.

41

Eyes

*A*part from the importance of having good light in a photograph, if you are taking a photo of a person or animal you also want to get what they call a catchlight in their eyes. It's that little sparkle of light reflected in their eyes. As an art teacher it was also one of the things I taught. A student would come up for some help and I'd tell them to put a little glimmer of light in the eyes and all of a sudden, the whole animal or person would look alive. It was amazing how that one little suggestion could change the whole look.

Matt 6:22 (NIV) says, "**The eye is the lamp of the body. If your eyes are healthy, your whole body will be full of light.**" What we look at affects how we reflect God's light.

Ps 16:8 (NIV) says, **"I keep my eyes always on the Lord. With him at my right hand, I will not be shaken."** Where we keep our focus gives stability to weather the hard times.

To me it is during the hard times that focus is even more important. 2 Cor 4:16-18 (NIV) says, **"Therefore we do not lose heart. Though outwardly we are wasting away, yet inwardly we are being renewed day by day. For our light and momentary troubles are achieving for us an eternal glory that far outweighs them all. So, we fix our eyes not on what is seen, but on what is unseen, since what is seen is temporary, but what is unseen is eternal."** It is easy to get discouraged with what is happening in the world around us but fixing our eyes on the eternal helps us gain the strength to deal

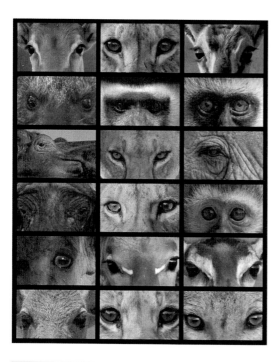

with the things that aren't.

Eph 1:18-19 (NIV) **"I pray that the eyes of your heart may be enlightened in order that you may know the hope to which he has called you, the riches of his glorious inheritance in his holy people, and his incomparably great power for us who believe."**

43

Childlike

While at the Selenkay Conservancy camp, a group of Vervet monkeys stopped in the heat of the afternoon to get a drink from a little watering pond there. Afterwards while the adults rested the young monkeys decided to use our vehicle like playground equipment. It always amazes me how young, whether animals or humans, seem to have endless energy. They chased each other around, slid down the front windshield and for some reason were licking it too. We weren't sure whether they were licking bugs or it was because of the reflection or some totally different reason. They were having fun with something we only thought of as a necessity to travel long distances. Those monkeys reminded me of little kids. Unlike adults, kids never tire of the smallest discovery and always see the magic in the ordinary.

The Bible tells, in Mark, that people were bringing children to Jesus and the disciples were rebuking them. Jesus was indignant and responded saying Mark 10:14-15 (NIV) "**Let the little children come to me, and do not hinder them, for the kingdom of God belongs to such as these. Truly I tell you, anyone who will not receive the kingdom of God like a little child will never enter it.**" When I think of what this means to be like a little child I think of things like their simple trust and their wide-eyed wonder. Things that are easy to lose while trying to have someone take you seriously as an adult. To me the best prescription for that seriousness is the wonder I have when I'm out in God's creation. I also

think singing songs to God helps. There is something about music that breaks through our adult defenses. Or better yet hang out with some kids and let their joy and endless energy rub off on you. Ps 65:8 (NIV) **"The whole earth is filled with awe at your wonders; where morning dawns, where evening fades, you call forth songs of joy."**

Hearing

I was awakened by a shriek, a sound that I can only describe as the sound of something dying, right outside my door. But then I had to rethink that because it continued randomly and at different places. I found out later that it was a Tree Hyrax, who is known for its loud vocalizations at night. On my first trip to Kenya the sound that stayed with me was waking up to the sound of hippos talking to each other in the river just outside my tent. It was a wonderful way to wake up. Another sound, which I heard on both trips, seemed to always be in the background, was the sound of Ring-necked Doves.

Hearing is a gift. I am so glad God created us to hear, see, smell, taste and touch. Can you imagine being without one of those senses? I find it interesting how the word hearing is used in Rom 10:17 (NIV) **"Consequently, faith comes from hearing the message, and the message is heard through the word about Christ."** Faith comes from hearing not reading or learning. Hearing requires our attention but not our effort like reading or learning would. Hearing means there's another person or persons involved to share the word about Christ. Now do I think this means a deaf person can't have faith, absolutely not but I do think it's an interesting choice of words to describe where faith comes from.

In Ps 116:1-2 the writer speaks of God hearing his cries, **"I love the Lord, for he heard my voice; he heard my cry for**

mercy. **Because he turned his ear to me, I will call on him as long as I live."** (NIV) I love the phrase "**turned his ear to me**." When we cry out to God he gives his full, gracious attention.

In Ps 65:8 **"The whole earth is filled with awe at your wonders; where morning dawns, where evening fades, you call forth songs of joy."** Those songs of joy can be from us but they are also from all the wonders God created in nature. As I write I'm hearing some birds which are singing out at my bird feeder. As you go through your day listen for those songs of joy and thank God for them.

Waiting

I had learned that Colobus monkeys would come through the property that I was staying at in Naivasha so I hoped that I would get to see them sometime during my visit. We saw some up close, at a neighbor's property, but they weren't doing anything but resting in the heat of the afternoon. So, I was still hoping I would get to see some when they were active. Each evening I would go sit on the deck waiting in hopes they would show up. On the 14th evening I noticed something white in the tree. I saw their tails first and then realized there was a group of them. It was interesting to see them eat and the young ones chasing each other around. As it got darker it really looked like they were going to spend the night, so I set my alarm to get up early to see if I could catch them in the morning too. Thankfully they were there around an hour before they headed out.

Photographing wildlife often involves a whole lot of waiting just for a few seconds or if you are lucky, minutes of action. Those waiting periods may seem a waste of time but often are as important as those few decisive moments. I don't know how many times I've waited for something and it didn't come but then I got something even better. Of course, there are those times that you wait and get nothing. Sometimes the time is spent figuring out the best position to get in so when something does come, I get a better shot.

Waiting is hard. We cry out to God that he will act quickly and in the way we want but what if the waiting is as important as the thing we are waiting for. One of the hardest things I've waited for was test results to come back when the results can mean life or death. The verses that meant the most to me during those long waiting periods are in Lam 3:22-26 (NIV) **"Because of the Lord's great love we are not consumed, for his compassions never fail. They are new every morning; great is your faithfulness I say to myself, 'The Lord is my portion; therefore I will wait for him.' The Lord is good to those whose hope is in him, to the one who seeks him; it is good to wait quietly for the salvation of the Lord."** I seldom got past that first line, "**Because of the Lord's great love we are not consumed.**" Sometimes you can't think past the moment you are in, so thinking about **"compassions that are new every morning"** just doesn't help that much but the idea of the Lord's love keeping us from being consumed was exactly what I needed to hear to make it to that next new morning.

Approaching God

While relaxing at a watering hole, watching elephants as the sun set, we noticed a mother elephant coming with two babies that looked very much the same size. We wondered if we were seeing twins, something really rare. Then all of a sudden, to our delight, one of the little ones started running as fast as it could to the elephants already at the watering hole. That's when we realized it was running to its mother. Evidently the other mother was "babysitting."

There were two things that made me smile about this encounter. First was the total abandon with which the young elephant ran to its mother. Second was when the baby got to its mom they touched and then of course soon after it began to nurse. That baby ran with confidence to its mother, just as we can run to the Father with confidence. Heb 4:16 (NIV) says, **"Let us then approach God's throne of grace with confidence, so that we may receive mercy and find grace to help us in our time of need."** It's that childlike faith along with God's mercy and grace that allow us to approach God, running to Him like the baby elephant.

The story of the prodigal son gives us yet another example as the son is coming back just hoping he could be a servant to his father. Luke 15:20 (NIV) says, **"So he got up and went to his father. But while he was still a long way off, his father saw him and was filled with compassion for him; he ran to**

his son, threw his arms around him and kissed him." The father not only welcomes him as his son but actually runs to meet him. This is the grace that we have been given. Grace that allows us to approach God with confidence.

Questions

Nature almost always leaves me with questions. Sometimes they can be answered but more often than not I have to accept that I will never know. The first evening I was in Naivasha I was in the backyard looking for birds to photograph. I saw a Cinnamon Bee-eater flying around and noticed there was a branch it favored, so I set up my camera. Never having seen this bird before I knew nothing of its behavior, so, everything I saw brought up questions. At one point I was excited to see it catch a bug and then go feed another bee-eater. I thought it could be a mate it was feeding but wasn't sure. Because it looked full grown, I didn't think it was a chick. The question was soon answered when the adult brought a dragonfly to the branch and two chicks soon followed. Waiting and watching long enough allowed me to get the answer to the question but other times the question never gets answered.

Why is it in this age of instant info and my need to have everything nailed down, with no questions left unanswered, do I so love the unpredictability of nature? I guess it's an exercise in letting go and realizing I am not in control of everything even if I think I can be in control of everything. It really goes back to original sin, the tree of the knowledge of good and evil. The need to know what God knew, rather than trust and not eat from the tree, really is more about control than knowledge. Nature provides me an opportunity to practice letting go of my perceived control and be okay with not knowing. Prov 3:5-6 (NIV) **"Trust in the Lord with all your heart and lean not on**

your own understanding; in all your ways submit to him, and he will make your paths straight."

I found this quote years ago that I have thought of many times since. "...have patience with everything unresolved in your heart and to try to love the questions themselves as if they were locked rooms or books written in a very foreign language. Don't search for the answers, which could not be given to you now, because you would not be able to live them. And the point is, to live everything. Live the questions now. Perhaps then, someday far in the future, you will gradually, without even noticing it, live your way into the answer."--Rainer Maria Rilke. If you wait long enough nature will sometimes give you the answers to the questions you have but with God we know we will eventually get the answers when we are face to face. 1 Cor 13:12 (NIV) **"For now we see only a reflection as in a mirror; then we shall see face to face. Now I know in part; then I shall know fully, even as I am fully known."** Until that time, we will have to trust the one who knows us fully.

Trees

When visiting an Eden camp, I got to watch the campers during a tree planting ceremony. I was told that the area when they first started planting trees was fairly barren. It wasn't until I saw a social media post recently that I got a clear idea of the transformation. (see photo next page, top) It is amazing the difference. I got a few photos of them planting but I was having difficulty because the undergrowth around the area was blocking the view. That's a good problem to have when you consider what it was like before.

Trees are valuable for many reasons. They purify our air as they produce the oxygen we need to breathe. They reduce the storm water runoff which helps with erosion which can pollute the waterways. Trees are homes for many species of wildlife and birds. The list could go on but needless to say they are an important part of our environment.

The Bible begins with two trees: the tree of life and the tree of the knowledge of good and evil. (Genesis 1 & 2) The Bible ends with trees in Rev 22:2 (NIV). **"On each side of the river stood the tree of life, bearing twelve crops of fruit, yielding its fruit every month. And the leaves of the tree are for the healing of the nations."** I haven't counted them but according to Matthew Sleeth, MD he says, "Other than people and God, trees are the most mentioned living thing in the Bible.

In Ps 1:2-3 says a tree is like the person, "**...whose delight is in the law of the Lord, and who meditates on his law day and**

EDEN CAMP REFORESTATION
2017 TO 2023

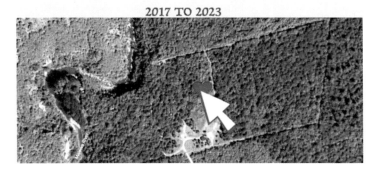

night. **That person is like a tree planted by streams of water, which yields its fruit in season and whose leaf does not wither—whatever they do prospers."** (NIV)

The verses I like the most are ones where trees take an active part in praising God. Ps 96:12 (NIV) "**...let all the trees of the forest sing for joy.**" And Isaiah 55:12 (NIV) "**You will go out in joy and be led forth in peace; the mountains and hills will burst into song before you, and all the trees of the field will clap their hands.**" Next time you see a tree let it remind you to sing for joy and clap your hands.

Big Steps

Have you ever taken a scary step out into something totally new? I watched what looked like a baby elephant's first step into the marshes at Amboseli. It leaned way out with its front feet to a dryer spot but realized it couldn't take such a long step. Then it tried to find a little piece of grass to stand on with one of its front feet while holding up one of its back feet to keep it from getting wet. This hesitation went on for quite some time but eventually it followed its mother into the marsh looking for higher ground wherever it could be found.

Stepping out in faith, doing something new, isn't always an easy thing. Even if it's something you know you want to do, it can still be scary. Remembering God's promises can help as you make those steps.

Promises to be with us and protect us. Isaiah 43:1-3 (NIV) **"Do not fear, for I have redeemed you; I have summoned you by name; you are mine. When you pass through the waters, I will be with you; and when you pass through the rivers, they will not sweep over you. When you walk through the fire, you will not be burned; the flames will not set you ablaze. For I am the Lord your God, the Holy One of Israel, your Savior."**

Promises to light the way.
Ps 119:105 (NIV) **"Your word is a lamp for my feet, a light on my path."**

Promises if we stumble to hold our hands. Ps 37:23-24 (NIV) **"The Lord makes firm the steps of the one who delights in him; though he may stumble, he will not fall, for the Lord upholds him with his hand.**

Expectations Vs. Expectant Hope

Wildlife photography has helped me define the difference between expectations and expectant hope. From the wildlife photography perspective, expectations are a list of things I believe I need to have a successful trip. Expectant hope would be going out and seeing what the day will bring knowing that if I am looking, I will experience wonder whether or not I get a good photograph.

There was a saying that I've heard from my elementary school teacher friends, "You get what you get, so, don't throw a fit." If I go out with expectations, I will almost always be disappointed. If I go out with expectant hope, I will almost always be surprised by something. Neither of those dispositions will change what I see that day because wildlife is by definition wild so there is no controlling it. What attitude I choose will change me.

It's not that all expectations are wrong, they are not, as a teacher I would tell my students my expectations. If my expectations for the day got interrupted, my attitude of expectant hope would have me looking for the teachable moments, which would often present themselves when obstacles arose.

For my trip to Kenya this year, instead of coming with a list of things I wanted to see I came with a goal of the type of photographs I wanted to take but it had nothing to do with which animal or bird it included. I wanted to take photos which

had interesting backgrounds, in good light and unusual perspectives. All of these were personal goals that I could work on with whatever was in front of my camera. And if I'm honest I really wanted to see Flamingos doing their mating dance but I knew that the odds were slim, so I tried not to hold that expectation. But that doesn't mean that I didn't go to places in hopes of seeing it. God was gracious and allowed me to see the Flamingos at Lake Elementiata where they hadn't been for several years.

This quote I found helpful in the differences between hope and expectation. "Having a hope helps us acknowledge that God knows best. Having an expectation often indicates that you know best. Having a hope produces a life of faith. Having an expectation produces a life of entitlement."—Thane Marcus

Hope allows Job to say, **"Though he slay me, yet will I hope in him."** Job 13:15 (NIV) Ps 62:5 (NIV) says, **"Yes, my soul, find rest in God; my hope comes from him."**

Birds of the Air

   Normally I don't focus on little birds to photograph. Not that I don't like them, but they are so hard to get because they are small and quick which makes catching a photo of them difficult. Early morning, being the most active time for birds, adds to the difficulty for me since I'm not a morning person. So, when I got up early to get little birds in Naivasha, I don't know how many photos I missed because I wasn't awake enough and my reaction time was too slow. This is why I prefer larger birds or animals but one thing is for sure those little birds aren't too small for God's attention. Matt 10:29-31 (NIV) **"Are not two sparrows sold for a penny? Yet not one of them will fall to the ground outside your Father's care. And even the very hairs of your head are all numbered. So don't be afraid; you are worth more than many sparrows."**

   God uses bird illustrations to give comfort. Ps 91:4 (NIV) says, **"He will cover you with his feathers, and under his wings you will find refuge; his faithfulness will be your shield and rampart."** David includes this idea in a prayer in Ps 17:8 (NIV) **"Keep me as the apple of your eye; hide me in the shadow of your wings."**

God also uses bird illustrations when addressing worry. He says, Matt 6:25-26 (NIV) **"Therefore I tell you, do not worry about your life, what you will eat or drink; or about your body, what you will wear. Is not life more than food, and the body more than clothes? Look at the birds of the air; they do not sow or reap or store away in barns, and yet your heavenly Father feeds them. Are you not much more valuable than they?"** When you see a bird today, use it as a reminder that God values you more and that he will provide refuge under his wings.

Digging Deeper

On my first trip to Kenya, we went to Samburu National Park. The river was dry but there were elephants in the dry river bed. As we watched we noticed an elephant swinging its front leg back and forth kicking sand. Our guide told us that the elephants dig deep, down to underground streams, to get water. It wasn't long before we could see they were drinking. The elephant's ability to find the water actually helps many other species that come after the elephants, drinking from the well they've dug. God has designed the elephants to be able to find the water which in turn benefits many more.

Jeremiah writes of a tree that has put down roots deep near a stream in Jer 17:7-8 (NIV) "**But blessed is the one who trusts in the Lord, whose confidence is in him. They will be like a tree planted by the water that sends out its roots by the stream. It does not fear when heat comes; its leaves are always green. It has no worries in a year of drought and never fails to bear fruit.**" Trust in God is something you choose to give, a step of faith. Each time you make a step of faith, digging deeper, it builds a confidence which won't be shaken. It allows you to "bear fruit" that others will benefit from in times of "drought."

What is the next step God is asking you to take? Where does He want you to dig deeper?

Moments

On the last day I was in Kenya I spent much of the afternoon trying to get my camera bag down to the weight allowance for Kenyan Airlines. It was quite a bit less than my arriving airline flight. After packing and weighing it several times taking more out each time I eventually got it down to as little weight as I could. Not long after, we decided to go out and see if we could find anything interesting in a plains area nearby, where there was wildlife. As I took my nicely packed camera equipment out, I was hoping that I wasn't wasting my time, wondering if we would get anything good as we went out. But one thing I've learned as a photographer is that you definitely won't have any chance to get something good if you don't go out, so out we went.

We actually had quite an interesting time watching sparing zebras for quite a while. Then as we were leaving the zebras, I was checking my list of things I wanted to photograph, for the ID book I was working on, and one I still needed was Pied Crows. No sooner had I said I need to get a Pied Crow than there were two just a short distance away. They were doing what we assume is a mating dance. It was fascinating to watch. Needless to say, the evening outing was worth unpacking my camera.

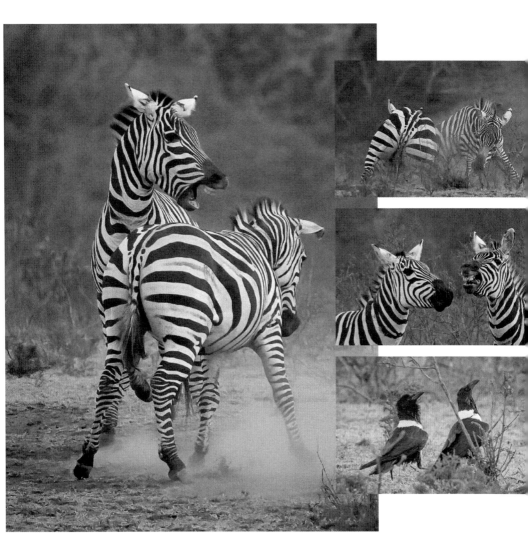

God uses nature to speak to us, to show his power and creativeness. He uses nature to speak for Him to people that have never even heard of him. Rom 1:20 (NIV) **"For since the creation of the world God's invisible qualities—his eternal power and divine nature—have been clearly seen, being understood from what has been made, so that people are without excuse."** How many will miss the opportunity because they aren't looking. As a school teacher I was always looking for that teachable moment and I think God gives us many teachable moments through nature as it reflects His divine nature. One thing is for sure, if we don't go out, we will miss some of those wonderful moments.

Made in the USA
Middletown, DE
30 September 2023

39840281R00038